Emb
Mit

EMBRACING STRESS:
A Daily Devotional for an Iambic Soul

MITCH COMSTOCK

First Edition 2015

Copyright © 2014. All rights reserved worldwide.
Contact Mitch Comstock for permission.
info@iambicsoul.com

www.iambicsoul.com

Scripture quotations are from The Holy Bible, English Standard Version® (ESV®), copyright © 2001 by Crossway, a publishing ministry of Good News Publishers. Used by permission. All rights reserved.

ISBN-13: 978-1511773539

ISBN-10: 1511773537

DEDICATION

To the one who I could truly never live without. My brother, Jesus. Thank you for your many gifts to me.

Acknowledgements

First I would like to thank you for reading this. My prayer is that this helps you find faith in a sure foundation.

I would like to thank my parents for their pursuit of God and their response to His pursuit of them.

I would like to thank my wife and children, they, like no one else, have helped me understand how loved I am and how sinful I am.

Jonathan, you brought me so much joy. I will always cherish our days together when you were just a baby.

Colt, you always bring a smile to me. I love learning to understand what goes on in your heart.

Samuel, your "Yes" reminds me of what I need to say to God on a daily basis.

Heath, I will always love the fact that you won't give me kisses, but that you cherish the ones that I give you.

Misti, your encouragement and gentleness with me never ceases to amaze or impress me. Thank you for listening and for respecting me when I don't deserve either.

Most importantly, I would like to thank the God of Abraham, Isaac and Moses. To the God of Israel and the God of David, thank you Creator for being my friend.

Table of Contents

Preliminaries 11
    What is an Iambic Soul? 12
    Who should use this book? 13
    How to Use This Book 14

Section 1: Confessions of an Iambic Soul 17
    Discover my heart 18
    My Pain 22
    Circumstances 26
    Far From Me 30
    My Righteousness 34
    A Rebel 38
    Misunderstood 42
    Rotten at the Core 46
    Father forgive me 50
    Foreigners 54
    My worship 58
    Me 62

Section 2: Cries of an Iambic Soul 67
    Longing 68
    A Squirmy Heart 72
    Emotions 76
    I Want to Know 80
    How Great Is Our Father's Love? 84
    Honesty 88

My Arms. 92
How Quickly 96
What Does Repentance Look Like? 100
Our Righteousness 104
My Heart 108
In Bed 112
Why, Why, Why? 116

Section 3: Redemption of an Iambic Soul 121
His Patience 122
Infection 126
Paid in Full 130
Alive 134
My all 138
What does it mean to pray? 142
End To These Troubles 146
I Know 150
Awakened 154
All in All 158
Christ Is Risen 162
Declared the King 166
Sin Forgiven 170

Conclusions 175
Final Thoughts 176
Afterword 178
About the Author 183

Preliminaries

What is an Iambic Soul?

The first question I get asked when I tell someone the full title of this book is, "What does iambic mean?"

The short answer is iambic refers to rhythms of unstressed and stressed syllables in poetry. I use it as a metaphor to describe the stressed and unstressed periods that my heart seems to go through. I used to think that only the unstressed times were good and that I shouldn't have any stress in my life, unless I was doing something wrong.

I now realize that both are necessary and planned parts of life. If stress is occuring that does not mean I am doing anything wrong. It simply means this world isn't what it was meant to be and that is a part of life in this temporary world.

Hopefully that helps you understand my declaration:

My name is Mitch Comstock. I am an iambic soul. I no longer rebel against the stress. I now embrace the rhythms of the unstressed and stressed times in my life and leave the results to God. His hand is good, and I can trust the stress that has a purpose. Even if that purpose is not for my own individual good. Even if I never see what that purpose is.

God is big enough. God is strong enough. God is smart enough. He is never tricked. He is never overpowered. He loves me. I can and will trust Him.

I hope you enjoy your time here, and I hope this book helps other iambic souls on their journey to find peace.

Who should use this book?

First, any individual who has experienced the tensions of stress in their life should find these conversations with God beneficial. Over the last few years I have dealt with the uncertainty that comes with seeing and trying to understand the nature of God's provision. These are my conversations with God surrounding my part and His part in this process. We have talked lots about my idols and about His majesty.

Secondly, any group of people looking to increase the depth of their relationship with Christ and each other should find in these pages food for thought deep enough and wide enough to provide interesting conversation. Hopefully, they will find answers within their soul that prove worth discovering.

Lastly, while I think this book should speak more to the established believer in Christ, it should reap benefits to any who take the time to read it and honestly examine their own soul.

How to Use This Book

This book is divided into three sections. Confessions, Cries and then Redemption of an Iambic Soul.

In the first section, Confessions of Iambic Soul, you will find an overall theme about the nature of man's sinfulness, specifically my own. Hopefully you will use this section to identify areas of your own sinfulness.

In the next section, Cries of an Iambic Soul, you will read about the desperate nature of our current earthly dilemma. This should help you identify our plight while we are here on this planet.

In the section Redemption of an Iambic Soul I write about the eternal and earthly provisions of a loving God towards sinful man. This leads us to a deeper appreciation for exactly what God has done for us.

There is some overlap and every passage may not fit perfectly into any section. But this order follows the nature of the gospel.

1. We are sinful.
2. We must recognize this and desire change.
3. God provided for our sinfulness by sending His son Jesus Christ to die on a cross in our stead.

The salvation available from Him alone breeds redemption like none other and shows grace like no other grace.

In each section you will find a dozen or so "lessons." Each lesson is made up of:

- A passage that I have written
- A passage or two from scripture
- A few questions to stir thought

I'd encourage you to take your time with each lesson. Read it again until you are convinced you are answering the questions honestly. For some lessons you may connect instantly. Others may take you more than one reading to get the most out of it.

This is because we all have different backgrounds and experiences. Things will strike you differently on different readings, even just a few days or weeks apart.

Most importantly this book has been designed to be flexible. You can use it however you see fit, but the intention was that you can grab a lesson and spend 15 minutes and get closer to God. At the very least, use these lessons to remind yourself about His nature.

We included the scripture passages so that this book would be self-contained. You can study it even when you don't have a Bible handy.

I would love it if you would share how you are using it. Feel free to reach out and connect with me.

Section 1: Confessions of an Iambic Soul

I long for things to be different, but reality is I keep my sins closer to me than my savior.

Discover my heart

How can I let you in?

How can I have you walk inside, when I know how dirty it is?

How can I know You and not desire to have You in, where all my dreams are and where I hide from the world and its evil?

How can I bring You in to the place I have sullied, bringing so much of the world's evil back with me and thrown it all around?

How can I let You see my sloppiness?

How can I not desire to see my heart different than it is? How can I not long for a heart more pure, more clean, more like someplace You would want to spend time?

Help me discover my heart and learn how to help You clean it up! Help me let You help me and not try to do it all myself. Help me as I am helpless. I am harassed.

You are my only hope. You are the only one who is truly there for me in my time of trial and tribulation. YOU are my joy, my hope, my song, my Redeemer, my King. YOU are my everything.

Prove me, O LORD, and try me; test my heart and my mind. For your steadfast love is before my eyes, and I walk in your faithfulness.

Psalm 26:2-3

When you examine your heart what do you find there?

How does it feel knowing that you are known completely, warts and all, by someone who cares enough to help you change?

Do you find yourself angry about past mistakes and ashamed of who you have been or what you have done?

What do you think God, who loved you enough to meet your greatest need, would say to you about your heart?

ಬಾಬಾಬಾಬಾಬಾಬಾಬಾಬಾಬಾ

Additional Notes

My Pain

is nothing compared to His.

Most of it comes from my own sins, my failure to trust Him.

All I do is wretched.

Nothing is persecuting me but me.

I don't know Him. I don't trust Him. I don't understand His ways. I long for things to be different, but reality is I keep my sins closer to me than my Savior. If I could only learn to let them, while never letting Him go.

When I look around me I see all the sin and all the weakness of those around me. I have no sympathy or compassion. I think to myself, "They will never change. They are doomed to repeat their sins and are stuck in their self-made tragedies."

Am I any different? Are those the words that I will be judged with? What does this say about how I truly feel about God? If I don't trust Him for them, does this say that I don't trust Him for me? Or that I don't believe His sufficiency for all?

Father grant mercy on me, a sinner. Show me your ways.

With what shall I come before the LORD, and bow myself before God on high? Shall I come before him with burnt offerings, with calves a year old? Will the LORD be pleased with thousands of rams, with ten thousands of rivers of oil? Shall I give my firstborn for my transgression, the fruit of my body for the sin of my soul? He has told you, O man, what is good; and what does the LORD require of you but to do justice, and to love kindness, and to walk humbly with your God?

Micah 6:6-8

For I desire steadfast love and not sacrifice, the knowledge of God rather than burnt offerings.

Hosea 6:6

How can I let mercy reign in my life?

When I am upset about sin in other's lives, am I more upset about the sin, its consequences, or how it affects me and/or those I care about?

How can I avoid passing judgment on others and step in as an instrument of grace in their lives without "approving" of obvious sin?

What is it that God desires most of me?

☙☙☙☙☙☙☙☙☙☙☙☙☙

Additional Notes

Circumstances

My life, my attitude and my soul are so caught up in circumstances. I wish I could explain it clearly, but my whole being stresses and strains with financial, social, relational, personal and physical trials.

I recognize both this and the fact that it should not be so. I should find something deeper. A firmer foundation. A sturdier anchor. A brighter light in the lighthouse. A better lamp for my path. A more accurate GPS.

My dependence on circumstances is sinful. It shows the priorities of my heart and the depravity of my soul.

As I write, I am so aware of who is greater, which path is truer, and where my only hope and salvation comes from. I recognize the likelihood of my heart dragging me back under the moment I leave the sanctuary. As my children scream for food and I raise my voice, and the moment I look hatefully at my wife because she reminds me that we can't "afford" the meal that my stomach desires, I am that sinful man.

Father please forgive me. Help me to trust You more and me less every day.

So when God desired to show more convincingly to the heirs of the promise the unchangeable character of his purpose, he guaranteed it with an oath, so that by two unchangeable things, in which it is impossible for God to lie, we who have fled for refuge might have strong encouragement to hold fast to the hope set before us. We have this as a sure and steadfast anchor of the soul, a hope that enters into the inner place behind the curtain, where Jesus has gone as a forerunner on our behalf, having become a high priest forever after the order of Melchizedek.

Hebrews 6:17-20

When was the last time you found yourself distracted and downcast by some situation in your life?

What does it look like when you trust God despite very uncomfortable circumstances?

If you could come up with any person in history to represent you and your concerns before God, who comes to mind? Do you think Christ would do a better job than them? Why?

Based on His willingness to sacrifice for you, what is something that matters more to Christ than you do?

ಬಾಬಾಬಾಬಾಬಾಬಾಬಾಬಾಬಾ

Additional Notes

Far From Me

You can be physically very close to someone and emotionally very distant.

Just like a husband and wife in the same bed after a fight, many in the pew are far from God. Unlike a husband and wife in the same bed after a fight, many in the pew are entirely unaware of the distance between them and their God.

The ironic thing is that regardless of our knowledge of our separation, we are all the same distance from God.

In a marriage, it takes two individuals traveling similar distances to become close again. With God we simply need to turn around and face Him again, and He will travel the whole distance for us.

When I think He is far from me, the evidence says that I am far from Him.

Father, open my eyes to my sin and draw me back in again. Help me become the man You desire me to be and change my wicked ways.

We must all die; we are like water spilled on the ground, which cannot be gathered up again. But God will not take away life, and he devises means so that the banished one will not remain an outcast.

2 Samuel 14:14

Can you think of a time in your life when you had a distant, broken or strained relationship with someone you loved?

How does it feel when someone you are close to doesn't behave in a loving manner or doesn't love you back?

Have you ever spent time trying to plot and plan how to repair one of these damaged relationships?

How does it make you feel knowing that God stayed up late last night figuring out how He could bring you back to Him?

಩಩಩಩಩಩಩಩಩಩಩಩

Additional Notes

My Righteousness

In my purest moments, I am true evil. I worship others and sacrifice my children on the altar of public opinion.

I have offered my wife as a burnt offering on the altar of my desire for her. I regularly sleep with prostitutes of praise from others. I give all my best possessions to the priests of the temple of me.

At its innermost place is a large idol made out of comfort and blessings. The idol's face is the one I see daily in the mirror.

I worship this god, and pray to him multiple times a day. I ask him to bless me, and I tell all who will listen how great I think he is.

He gives me the pleasures of feeling good about myself in exchange for my wife, my family, all my worldly possessions and my immortal soul. He whispers great praises to me when I sleep, and tells me how wonderful I am when compared to others.

I have looked at the gods of others, but none of them make me feel as good as mine one does. I've already sacrificed and given up so much to the altar of me.

I just can't admit that I was wrong and that this god has no power at all. But I have come to recognize this deep down inside. I must change my behavior to ever have a chance of being satisfied for even a moment.

Father please forgive me. Cleanse me with fire. Remove my impurities and let me love and trust in Your everlasting arms.

O Lord, open my lips, and my mouth will declare your praise. For you will not delight in sacrifice, or I would give it; you will not be pleased with a burnt offering. The sacrifices of God are a broken spirit; a broken and contrite heart, O God, you will not despise.

Psalms 51:15-17

Do you struggle to admit that you are broken? Is there any part of you that feels like you are "not that bad?"

How do the opinions of others shape and control you?

What does your own selfishness look like?

What would a broken and contrite heart look like in your life?

Additional Notes

A Rebel

I rebel in my heart, mind, spirit, soul and physical body. All of me looks to me. I should recognize by now that Christ is the one who makes me and makes anything that I desire better.

Trusting in Him with my whole heart is easy to sing and hard to do. I sing about crowning Him Lord of All, yet treat Him as though He is merely a steward of MY throne, a counselor or trusted advisor.

The wisest advisors quit giving advice when it is repeatedly ignored. And kings don't bow to their stewards.

I am guilty of treason. I take what is entrusted in me and treat it as though it is all mine. I plan what I will do next, how I will behave and what actions I choose.

If I am to trust in Him with my WHOLE heart, then I must not trust at all in my own self. The wisdom He has given me, the strategic mind, the physical strength, all of my giftedness is a part of my problem. How can I trust in the gift when there is a much greater Gift-Giver to trust in?

Help me to learn today, Lord what it means to trust in You with my WHOLE heart.

He. Teach me, O LORD, the way of your statutes; and I will keep it to the end. Give me understanding, that I may keep your law and observe it with my whole heart. Lead me in the path of your commandments, for I delight in it. Incline my heart to your testimonies, and not to selfish gain! Turn my eyes from looking at worthless things; and give me life in your ways. Confirm to your servant your promise, that you may be feared. Turn away the reproach that I dread, for your rules are good. Behold, I long for your precepts; in your righteousness give me life!

Psalms 119:33-40

What has been the results of half-hearted trust of yourself or others in your life?

What is required in order to have whole-hearted trust in another? What is an obstacle to whole-heartedness for you?

Does a king become less royal when one of his subjects refuses to recognize his authority? How does the submission of his subjects impact his kingliness?

What should our response be to one so important, so powerful, so concerned about our well-being?

ಆಒಆಒಆಒಆಒಆಒಆಒಆಒಆಒ

Additional Notes

Misunderstood

How quick am I to judge others and their intentions. I am so sure what their motivation is and I can see right through them. I know what they say, and I know what they really mean.

Ironic that I often feel misunderstood and judged by others. Some have written me off as a goody-two-shoes. Some have judged me as weird. Some think I am insincere. Many assume that they know what my reaction would be before they even bother to communicate anything with me.

I live with my dichotomies. Ironic even more is that I sing regularly that I am going to follow Christ no matter what, yet I regularly look at the world I live in and tell myself that I know best about what "should" have happened.

I judge Christ and tell Him what He should do in my life so often. He should give me this or that or protect me from this or that. I find my intelligence and intuition work against me when it comes to worshipping God and trusting Him.

Father please forgive me daily. I am often critical of everything from Your provision to Your timing. Help me accept Your authorship and loving hand in my life and in the lives of those around me.

Humble yourselves, therefore, under the mighty hand of God so that at the proper time he may exalt you, casting all your anxieties on him, because he cares for you. Be sober-minded; be watchful. Your adversary the devil prowls around like a roaring lion, seeking someone to devour. Resist him, firm in your faith, knowing that the same kinds of suffering are being experienced by your brotherhood throughout the world. And after you have suffered a little while, the God of all grace, who has called you to his eternal glory in Christ, will himself restore, confirm, strengthen, and establish you. To him be the dominion forever and ever. Amen.

1 Peter 5:6-11

How does our humility impact our desire to judge others and for us to control all aspects of our life?

According to Peter, why should we entrust or cast our cares on/to God?

As we struggle with our flesh (inside) and our adversary (outside), what brings us through it?

What is the significance of the four things that verse 10 says Christ personally wants to accomplish in you? Are there any of them that make you nervous?

ఌఌఌఌఌఌఌఌఌఌఌఌ

Additional Notes

Rotten at the Core

How wicked and evil is my heart? I sit and look at others, and their wickedness is obvious. Mine is more deceptive. I say nice things to others and mean none of them.

All I really care about is myself. I look for opportunities to look important and selfless, yet I am full of myself and as selfish as anyone that I judge as unworthy.

My belly is constantly hungry. My greed knows no bounds. My desires control me.

Indeed my sin knows no bounds.

And somehow this is okay. Somehow You have made me righteous. Somehow You are able to not only both cover over my past and current iniquity, but also purify my future heart so that there will be a day when I will be pure.

How great and awesome is Your love? Your mercy is new every morning. You rule with a righteous hand. Thank You for Your grace, mercy, strength and justice.

But you, beloved, building yourselves up in your most holy faith and praying in the Holy Spirit, keep yourselves in the love of God, waiting for the mercy of our Lord Jesus Christ that leads to eternal life. And have mercy on those who doubt; save others by snatching them out of the fire; to others show mercy with fear, hating even the garment stained by the flesh. Now to him who is able to keep you from stumbling and to present you blameless before the presence of his glory with great joy, to the only God, our Savior, through Jesus Christ our Lord, be glory, majesty, dominion, and authority, before all time and now and forever. Amen.

Jude 1:20-25

What should be your part in striving towards your own holiness? God's part?

What does it look like to have mercy on those who doubt? Does that include yourself?

How could you snatch them out of the fire?

According to Jude, who is able to keep us from stumbling? How does that make you feel?

ಞಞಞಞಞಞಞಞಞಞಞಞ

Additional Notes

Father forgive me.

My heart is not at all like yours.

I long for and constantly look for sacrifices that do not truly require sacrifice. I love to sacrifice on public altars and regularly give up things that do not matter to me.

I cling to things that are not healthy. I love things that are worldly and not eternal.

Change my heart and help my hands know what sacrifice looks like for me. I am afraid to get my hands dirty – afraid to get wet. I desire comfort, warmth and wealth more than I care about what matters to You.

Father forgive my inactivity. Father, convict and convince me. Father, I desire for You to help me let You change me. Lead me in your ways everlasting.

Guard your steps when you go to the house of God. To draw near to listen is better than to offer the sacrifice of fools, for they do not know that they are doing evil. Be not rash with your mouth, nor let your heart be hasty to utter a word before God, for God is in heaven and you are on earth. Therefore let your words be few.

Ecclesiastes 5:1-2

In the meantime, when so many thousands of the people had gathered together that they were trampling one another, he began to say to his disciples first, Beware of the leaven of the Pharisees, which is hypocrisy. Nothing is covered up that will not be revealed, or hidden that will not be known. Therefore whatever you have said in the dark shall be heard in the light, and what you have whispered in private rooms shall be proclaimed on the housetops.

Luke 12:1-3

Why does God hate public sacrifices?

Is it really the right thing if it is done for the wrong reason?

Make a list of some right reasons and some wrong reasons to do good.

How does the thought that every thing you've done in secret will be revealed in public make you feel?

Who do you know that can help you keep your actions rightly motivated?

ଔଔଔଔଔଔଔଔଔଔଔଔ

Additional Notes

Foreigners

What gods tempt my soul? What do I feel myself admiring? Where does my heart love to live?

Riches, the admiration of others, my feeling or need to feel superior (or at least accepted). I constantly struggle with dueling desires to be special and to be normal.

The more normal I feel, the more I desire to be special. The more special others treat me, the more I desire to be normal.

I think at the root of both is an issue with loneliness. We think we would be more popular (and possibly less alone) if we were special. We also think that if we could fit in and be normal, we would be less alone.

Both desires are consumed with what others think of me!

How do I live with the things that will be with me while I walk on this planet, but not worship them?

I must learn to lean on Him, and see my true salvation in Him alone.

In you, O LORD, do I take refuge; let me never be put to shame! In your righteousness deliver me and rescue me; incline your ear to me, and save me! Be to me a rock of refuge, to which I may continually come; you have given the command to save me, for you are my rock and my fortress. Rescue me, O my God, from the hand of the wicked, from the grasp of the unjust and cruel man. For you, O Lord, are my hope, my trust, O LORD, from my youth. Upon you I have leaned from before my birth; you are he who took me from my mother's womb. My praise is continually of you.

Psalms 71:1-6

If you had to name the other gods in your life, what would their names be?

Do you ever struggle with loneliness? Do you find yourself more often struggling with the desire to be special or the desire to be normal?

How does faith in God help us treat others as special? As normal?

What does taking refuge in God look like in your life?

Additional Notes

My worship

All my efforts to praise God are filled with selfishness, empty promises and conceit.

I do not love You; not by my actions.

I do not surrender all; really I don't even surrender most.

I have really decided to follow my wicked heart and will do whatever good things man can see.

I worship relationships and the praise of man. I desire nothing more than to fill my belly and to be told that is okay.

I judge others and condemn their actions, especially Your children.

My best efforts at worship wilt in seconds and are rotten at their core.

Forgive my unfaithfulness and the sins that surround me in my constant denials.

I desire to love You with my heart and soul, and know that I can't succeed without Your help. Thank you for Your grace, mercy and justice.

Thus, when you give to the needy, sound no trumpet before you, as the hypocrites do in the synagogues and in the streets, that they may be praised by others. Truly, I say to you, they have received their reward. But when you give to the needy, do not let your left hand know what your right hand is doing, so that your giving may be in secret. And your Father who sees in secret will reward you. And when you pray, you must not be like the hypocrites. For they love to stand and pray in the synagogues and at the street corners, that they may be seen by others. Truly, I say to you, they have received their reward. But when you pray, go into your room and shut the door and pray to your Father who is in secret. And your Father who sees in secret will reward you.

Matthew 6:2-6

What do your actions reveal about your praise of God?

In what ways do you find yourself struggling with the praise or disdain of man?

What does Christ say in Matthew about the dangers of doing the right things (prayer, giving to the needy, etc.) for the wrong reasons?

What are some of the ways that God has shown you that He loves you? What is His promise at the end of the passage about those who seek Him for the right reasons?

ಌಌಌಌಌಌಌಌಌಌಌಌ

Additional Notes

Me

In the midst of whatever I am involved in, I am SO in the way.

My way is so self-serving. In my most selfless moment, I am so proud of how good I am.

God uses me always, (and in all ways), in spite of me, not because of or through me.

Father, I confess my sin of selfishness. Please keep using me in spite of me. I am blown away by the vastness and sovereign nature of Your plan.

Your ways are not my ways. Help me to live a Philippians 2 lifestyle. Thank you for all Your goodness and the chance to see You move.

For I do not understand my own actions. For I do not do what I want, but I do the very thing I hate. Now if I do what I do not want, I agree with the law, that it is good. So now it is no longer I who do it, but sin that dwells within me. For I know that nothing good dwells in me, that is, in my flesh. For I have the desire to do what is right, but not the ability to carry it out. For I do not do the good I want, but the evil I do not want is what I keep on doing. Now if I do what I do not want, it is no longer I who do it, but sin that dwells within me. So I find it to be a law that when I want to do right, evil lies close at hand. For I delight in the law of God, in my inner being, but I see in my members another law waging war against the law of my mind and making me captive to the law of sin that dwells in my members. Wretched man that I am! Who will deliver me from this body of death? Thanks be to God through Jesus Christ our Lord! So then, I myself serve the law of God with my mind, but with my flesh I serve the law of sin.

Romans 7:15-25

Can you think of a time that you got in your own way?

What do you do to try and combat selfishness in your own life?

Who is the least selfish person that you know?

How do you feel when you are around them?

How does Christ's sacrifice for us show His love for us? What do you think our response should be to Him?

ଓଃଓଃଓଃଓଃଓଃଓଃଓଃଓଃଓଃଓଃ

Additional Notes

ଓଃଓଃଓଃଓଃଓଃଓଃଓଃଓଃଓଃଓଃ

Section 2: Cries of an Iambic Soul

Every one of my righteous deeds feels wicked at its core.

Longing

I long for heaven, yet I admit my unworthiness. Even what little I understand of heaven shows me how completely the earth corrupts.

I find it unsatisfying to say that death has no sting when some will remain in torment.

I find it unsatisfying to say that I am pardoned for what He has done. My sins are so immense, I cannot stand in His presence. He can only look at me through Christ-colored glasses.

I long for things to be different. For the washing of my sins to be permanent. For them to be removed from me instantly. For me not to sit in them in the moments that I feign worship.

Help me, father. All my dissatisfaction in this is still sin. You reign completely, and Your Word is absolutely correct and pure.

Your ways are not mine. And I am not equipped to even begin to understand them.

But that is not the way you learned Christ! — assuming that you have heard about him and were taught in him, as the truth is in Jesus, to put off your old self, which belongs to your former manner of life and is corrupt through deceitful desires, and to be renewed in the spirit of your minds, and to put on the new self, created after the likeness of God in true righteousness and holiness.

Ephesians 4:20-24

Every believer in Christ should have a healthy level of dissatisfaction in their own sin. What are some sins of your own that you still struggle with? (If you can't come up with anything here ask a parent, spouse or close loved one for help.)

What are the three steps Paul gives in Ephesians 4 to living like Christ?

In what ways can you put off your old self? Put on your new self?

What are some practical steps to renewing your mind?

Additional Notes

A Squirmy Heart

I have a practice of whispering in the ears of my children. I pull them close as to tell them a secret and then tell them with a whisper, "Your daddy loves you."

I did this today at church with my four-year-old, and he responded softly, "Your son loves you." And melted my heart. We then proceeded to hug as deep a hug as I have ever given or received.

It lasted for all of 5 seconds, but it gave me a joy that is still welling up in me. It ended because he got squirmy, like a four-year-old is bound to do.

As our moment was ending, I heard the words of the song we were singing and realized how similar God's love is for us and how similar my heart is to a four-year-old.

God longs for us to cling to Him and to seek His face. Whenever we do so, it lasts for mere seconds; He desires that we never let go.

Help me, Lord, love You longer and heal my squirmy heart that is easily distracted from things that truly matter.

With my whole heart I seek you; let me not wander from your commandments! I have stored up your word in my heart, that I might not sin against you.

Psalms 119:10-11

What are the things in your life that distract you and make you want to get out of your Father's lap?

Describe how you feel when you think about how much love you have for your children.

Describe how you feel when you think about being loved that much by someone or something else.

What practices or habits can you start that will make spending time with God pleasant and more frequent?

ൟൟൟൟൟൟൟൟൟൟൟ

Additional Notes

Emotions

Why do these feelings rule me?

It takes nothing to change them. I won't consider doing something when I'm in a bad mood that I would normally do gladly in a good mood and vice versa.

It affects my marriage, my parenting, my work, my religion, me.

Emotions rule, and it requires a constant reminding my mind that the emotions are not foundational. You can only build a foundation on truth. Truth isn't the roof over your head, but it will keep your house from falling in the storm.

Help me forget the circumstances that direct me. Show me how to control my emotions and live in the truth of the impending joy that You have promised Yours.

Help me get over finances, arguments, my desires for praise, peace and happiness. Help me live like You did and trust You, even when I don't feel like it.

You are worthy; Your love is sufficient. You are strong, and You meet all needs for all Your children. You are the only One that is stable and can be safely trusted.

Keep your life free from love of money, and be content with what you have, for he has said, "I will never leave you nor forsake you." So we can confidently say, "The Lord is my helper; I will not fear; what can man do to me?"

Hebrews 13:5-6

Why do you think God says to His people over and over again, "I will never leave you or forsake you?"

What are some of the things and circumstances that seem to control you?

How does understanding that God is loving, powerful and knowledgeable enough to overcome your problems make you feel?

Who is someone in your life that you will pray for Christ to reveal this nature to?

Additional Notes

I Want To Know

I want to know that I am following your will. That you are pleased with me. That I do right, and all this is sinful. This is me trying to do it all.

I need to be comfortable in my own sinful skin. Not the kind of comfortable that stays in one spot, but the kind that stands before the judge and admits the truth. GUILTY. The kind of comfortable that accepts mercy and acknowledges the need for it without the accompanying, "You won't regret this." "I'll make you proud," or whatever other sinful comment makes me feel a little bit better.

I need to be comfortable enough to accept where God has me (as opposed to where I am) in the sanctification process, without being the kind of comfortable that is unwilling to change or to participate in the process. The Spirit convicts, but we must go to Nineveh.

To be wholly dissatisfied with my sin is to be dissatisfied with God. I must accept that while on the planet, I will always be sinful, yet not be willing to just "accept" my sin. My efforts to change must be eternally couched in the praise, trust and admiration of the One truly able to cause change.

Thank you Father for Christ's righteousness imputed on me.

Trust in the LORD with all your heart, and do not lean on your own understanding. In all your ways acknowledge him, and he will make straight your paths. Be not wise in your own eyes; fear the LORD, and turn away from evil.

Proverbs 3:5-7

What are some ways that you have struggled in knowing the will of the Lord?

What do you think acknowledging God in all your ways looks like in your life?

How do you attempt to strike the balance between grace and justice when looking at your own personal sin?

Is there any action you can take today to get real about your sin and to trust God more while striving to change?

ఌఌఌఌఌఌఌఌఌఌఌఌ

Additional Notes

How Great Is Our Father's Love?

I sit in worship next to my son and struggle to imagine something more precious to me than his desire to sit next to me. He does nothing and says nothing as he reaches over and puts his tiny hand in mine.

My delight in his desire to spend time with me is immense.

How inferior am I to a God who was powerful enough to create the universe and loving enough to take the shape of man? He submitted himself to mocking and torture by some of those that He created, so that He could save some of them.

Scripture over and over again expresses His delight in those who seek His face. Based on my reaction to my son's desire to spend time with me, I think I finally understand slightly how that feels.

And you, Solomon my son, know the God of your father and serve him with a whole heart and with a willing mind, for the LORD searches all hearts and understands every plan and thought. If you seek him, he will be found by you, but if you forsake him, he will cast you off forever.

1 Chronicles 28:9

Seek the LORD while he may be found; call upon him while he is near; let the wicked forsake his way, and the unrighteous man his thoughts; let him return to the LORD, that he may have compassion on him, and to our God, for he will abundantly pardon. For my thoughts are not your thoughts, neither are your ways my ways, declares the LORD. For as the heavens are higher than the earth, so are my ways higher than your ways and my thoughts than your thoughts.

Isaiah 55:6-9

And without faith it is impossible to please him, for whoever would draw near to God must believe that he exists and that he rewards those who seek him.

Hebrews 11:6

What do you think about when you are told to seek the Lord? Where do you seek Him? What do you do when you find Him?

How important do you feel when you think about the fact that the Creator of the Universe desires to spend time with you?

How often do you sit and just ask God to help you see His face? How many minutes of silence do you spend with God?

What is something practical that you could do today to seek the Lord?

☙☙☙☙☙☙☙☙☙☙☙☙

Additional Notes

Honesty

When I sit in honesty with my thoughts and feelings, I find fear, shame, grief and regret.

When you are young, the future is nothing but hopes and dreams. As you age, you become more and more accepting of what is and live in the reality of what things have become.

When you are young, life is full of promise and full of potential. As you get older, you find yourself loaded down with baggage that you never intended to create; dreams become something that just help you cope.

For most of us, the past is either where we remember fondly all the promise we once had or it is the place where we try and forget how we birthed all our current pains. Or both.

And yet reality is so different than my thoughts and feelings portray.

When I remember my Savior and sit in honesty with my thoughts and feelings, I find myself grateful. I am forgiven, loved, changed, redeemed, and full of grace, hope and love.

The future is not a hopeful thing; it is a certain thing.

The difference is dramatic, and all that is needed is to recall the One who truly loves me.

Thank you Jesus for a future that is filled with hope and no regard or regrets for my past!

Oh give thanks to the LORD, for he is good, for his steadfast love endures forever! Let the redeemed of the LORD say so, whom he has redeemed from trouble and gathered in from the lands, from the east and from the west, from the north and from the south. Some wandered in desert wastes, finding no way to a city to dwell in; hungry and thirsty, their soul fainted within them. Then they cried to the LORD in their trouble, and he delivered them from their distress. He led them by a straight way till they reached a city to dwell in. Let them thank the LORD for his steadfast love, for his wondrous works to the children of man! For he satisfies the longing soul, and the hungry soul he fills with good things. Some sat in darkness and in the shadow of death, prisoners in affliction and in irons, for they had rebelled against the words of God, and spurned the counsel of the Most High. So he bowed their hearts down with hard labor; they fell down, with none to help. Then they cried to the LORD in their trouble, and he delivered them from their distress. He brought them out of darkness and the shadow of death, and burst their bonds apart. Let them thank the LORD for his steadfast love, for his wondrous works to the children of man!

Psalms 107:1-15

As you look back on your life, what are your biggest memories, emotions and feelings about your life? Were any of these areas filled with hope in the past? Pain?

Do you have a friend who has baggage that you wish that they would give over to God?

Are you close enough to them to explain it to them and share your experiences with them?

Is there anything else you need to deal with in your own life?

ಌಌಌಌಌಌಌಌಌಌಌಌ

Additional Notes

My Arms

Are too short. My wingspan too narrow.

Lord, you have blessed me with children so that I may understand how You love me.

You have blessed me with many, so I can understand how insufficient my abilities are.

I desire to stretch my arms wider. To love children who aren't my own. To protect them from the world around them. And I am completely unable.

Yet I find this truth reliable: the more children I am responsible for, the more I let down.

Your love never fails. Your gifts never stop giving. Your fountain never runs dry. What You plan always comes to fruition. Thank You for showing me my inadequacies, because they make me so aware of the lack of them in You.

Blessed be the God and Father of our Lord Jesus Christ, who has blessed us in Christ with every spiritual blessing in the heavenly places, even as he chose us in him before the foundation of the world, that we should be holy and blameless before him. In love he predestined us for adoption as sons through Jesus Christ, according to the purpose of his will, to the praise of his glorious grace, with which he has blessed us in the Beloved. In him we have redemption through his blood, the forgiveness of our trespasses, according to the riches of his grace, which he lavished upon us, in all wisdom and insight making known to us the mystery of his will, according to his purpose, which he set forth in Christ as a plan for the fullness of time, to unite all things in him, things in heaven and things on earth.

Ephesians 1:3-10

What significance do you find in the truth that God chose you?

Describe your "normal" response to God's lavish blessings for you?

How does your view of your parents and their provision impact your view of God?

Does the comparison of love for family help or hinder your view of just how highly God thinks of you?

What is one thing you can do today to share the love that God has lavished on you with someone else?

Additional Notes

How Quickly

Does my mind change?

Why am I so circumstantially motivated?

I find life so much happier when there is a little bit extra money left over after the bills are paid.

Life seems to be brighter and the world better when I have 5 minutes extra free time before I have to be anywhere.

Why do I let time and money and the rest of the problems of this world, weigh me down and affect my countenance?

Is my God less present when my schedule full? Or my pocket empty?

My sinful flesh demands its own way in order to be happy.

What has been handed to me is enough. His grace is sufficient. My debt is paid. I am covered, forgiven, loved on, cared for, watched over and provided for. For me to be dissatisfied is unappreciative.

Lord, help me feel the love that You have surrounded me with and covered me with even when my circumstances try to steal my joy. Help me smile when anything and everything comes my way. Your grace is more than enough for me.

I rejoiced in the Lord greatly that now at length you have revived your concern for me. You were indeed concerned for me, but you had no opportunity. Not that I am speaking of being in need, for I have learned in whatever situation I am to be content. I know how to be brought low, and I know how to abound. In any and every circumstance, I have learned the secret of facing plenty and hunger, abundance and need. I can do all things through him who strengthens me.

Philippians 4:10-13

What does Paul say is worse – having abundance or being needy?

Have you ever struggled with abundance? Being in need?

What got you through your struggles?

What is one circumstance that seems to dominate your thoughts right now?

How do we find contentment and peace at the moment of our struggle?

ॐॐॐॐॐॐॐॐॐॐॐॐ

Additional Notes

What Does Repentance Look Like?

Scripture tells me that repentance is a sign of salvation. What does that look like? How can we go and sin no more? Where does that power come from? What does that feel like? What does a repentant heart smell like? Why is it, 30+ years later, my heart still feels like rotting flesh?

I feel the God-shaped vacuum as much today as any day I ever have. I long for a day when sanctification is completed, and I am holy, set apart and fully devoted to Him. Yet today that seems so elusive. It is so easy to see my sin now, yet so hard to turn from it. In my youth, it seemed so hard to see it and easy to turn from when I saw it. I wonder how blind I was and why improved vision doesn't automatically reflect a renewed heart or a changed life.

I think what I am saying is, I am entirely dissatisfied with every ounce of my own righteousness; every one of my righteous deeds feels wicked at its core. I long to be filled with His righteousness. I long for heaven, when my joy will be made complete as the fullness of His sanctification in my life is fulfilled. I also long to see the glory of His sanctification in the lives of wicked men throughout the earth.

I long for what God has already done. I yearn to see it fully accomplished. I have come to understand that while here on this planet, I influence my present sanctification process; yet I know that ultimately and for eternity I have no part in it.

But do not overlook this one fact, beloved, that with the Lord one day is as a thousand years, and a thousand years as one day. The Lord is not slow to fulfill his promise as some count slowness, but is patient toward you, not wishing that any should perish, but that all should reach repentance. But the day of the Lord will come like a thief, and then the heavens will pass away with a roar, and the heavenly bodies will be burned up and dissolved, and the earth and the works that are done on it will be exposed. Since all these things are thus to be dissolved, what sort of people ought you to be in lives of holiness and godliness. . .

2 Peter 3:8-11

What are some things from which you have found yourself needing to repent?

What are some of the things that you find dissatisfying about living in this world?

According to Peter, what is the purpose of God's patience?

How do you think you would feel if you realized that God "delayed" Christ's second coming, so that you were able to come to know Him?

What is one practical thing that you can do today, to show Christ your repentance?

ಌಌಌಌಌಌಌಌಌಌಌಌ
Additional Notes

Our Righteousness

We must not JUST repent of our sins, but ALSO repent of our righteousness. We must have Christ completely substitute for us. If we receive only His sinlessness and not also His righteousness, we do not have enough to inherit heaven.

There is no other place for us in eternity but heaven or hell. You are not only saved from the one but also rewarded with the other; cast out of the one and then sent to the other.

We must lose all of our own righteousness in order to receive all of His.

Father, help me to trust with my whole heart in Your provision through Christ.

Brothers, my heart's desire and prayer to God for them is that they may be saved. For I bear them witness that they have a zeal for God, but not according to knowledge. For, being ignorant of the righteousness of God, and seeking to establish their own, they did not submit to God's righteousness. For Christ is the end of the law for righteousness to everyone who believes.

Romans 10:1-4

Can you remember the last time that you were proud of doing something nice for someone else?

How often are you motivated to do good simply because you just know it's the "right thing" to do?

Why do we need not just Christ's sinlessness but also His righteousness in order for us to be saved?

Are there any of your good deeds that you need to repent of and quit holding on to so tightly?

Additional Notes

My Heart

Why do our hearts fail us so frequently? I'm not talking about physically. The world tells us that no matter what we should trust our hearts, yet I find my heart is so fickle.

Hearts are influenced so much by circumstances. I am swayed by any light breeze. There is no stability in trusting a heart.

My heart believes every first impression, it loves con-men and infomercials. It loves compliments and cares about the eyes of men so much more than is healthy.

My heart is persuasive. It tells my mind what to think, and my mind is surprisingly easily deceived by its lies.

There is something deeper than my heart. There is something that longs for true truth. When my heart is failing my God stands firm.

Nevertheless, I am continually with you; you hold my right hand. You guide me with your counsel, and afterward you will receive me to glory. Whom have I in heaven but you? And there is nothing on earth that I desire besides you. My flesh and my heart may fail, but God is the strength of my heart and my portion forever. For behold, those who are far from you shall perish; you put an end to everyone who is unfaithful to you. But for me it is good to be near God; I have made the Lord GOD my refuge, that I may tell of all your works.

Psalms 73:23-28

Can you remember when someone gave you the advice to follow your heart? What was the situation prompting that advice?

Have you ever made a mistake in following your heart? Have you ever been too nice, or waited too long to confront someone?

What are some ways that your heart has lied to you?

What are some practical things you can do to make sure that God is the strength of your heart?

Why does the psalmist say that he has made God his refuge?

Who will you share the works of the Lord in your life with today?

In Bed

I sit and listen to the cosmos, pulling ideas from the ether. The clock dongs 12 times, and I think.

Thoughts spinning, family sleeping, mind racing with itself, and I find I must write.

What is inside must get out. What is outside demands attention.

I cannot begin to explain. I do not understand, yet I see wisdom and understanding sitting next to foolishness and confusion.

There is truth, and it hides. Darkness reigns inside. I try to fight and instead hide. It is hard to swallow pride.

I choose to trust what I cannot see, yet my heart tells me must be.

Father, Spirit, Friend, help this night to end. I long to be known, yet when I examine within, all I know is that I am unsure of what I find.

This truth I know: while I can't trust me, I can trust Him.

Will tomorrow bring an answer? Ask Him and see. I listen to the melody of sleep and know that tomorrow brings, peace.

I rejoin the machine and slumber. Zzz

Jesus said to him, "Have you believed because you have seen me? Blessed are those who have not seen and yet have believed." Now Jesus did many other signs in the presence of the disciples, which are not written in this book; but these are written so that you may believe that Jesus is the Christ, the Son of God, and that by believing you may have life in his name.

John 20:29-31

Why does John say all of Jesus' miracles were written in scripture?

What is an area where you feel darkness reigns inside in your life?

What do you think it will take to shine light on the darkness?

What is one thing that your pride won't let you admit to others?

How can Christ help you with this area?

☙☙☙☙☙☙☙☙☙☙☙☙

Additional Notes

Why, Why, Why?

Why is my heart so easily distracted by circumstances? I love God, but it seems to feel like that love is more real when my bills are paid and my relationships are even keeled.

Father, why, why, why?

My week fades and the next week comes into view...

My fickle heart forgets last week's provisions and gazes hesitantly at the giants in the valley.

Please help me to remember You daily and to trust in You and not in comfortable circumstances.

Hallelujah, glory be to You my great God!

Father, help me love You all my days and in all my ways with the same passion, emotion and fervor.

In all circumstances take up the shield of faith, with which you can extinguish all the flaming darts of the evil one . . .

Ephesians 6:16

What are some of your biggest distractions?

Write down some the biggest things God has provided for you.

Can you speak of how God can/does provide for you or eliminated your biggest distractions?

How do we find the secret of facing issues in life?

How can we point others to this?

Additional Notes

Section 3: Redemption of an Iambic Soul

It should also comfort us on a cosmic level that our provision is infinitely larger

His Patience

This morning I had issues with one if my sons, which required me to display great patience with him.

While in my heart, there was a part that desired to not have to "deal" with him, there was a much larger part that simply desired his best interests.

I saw how he was going to struggle the rest of life, if he didn't get resolution and learn how to live his life differently. Indeed, more than his actions, I saw his heart that needed changing.

This made my "sacrifice" very easy to bear. It was as I realized this that I thought of a different father who was willing to sacrifice so much more than time in order to help us with so much more than our behavior.

As I reflect on this, while being more than impressed by what He did, I look into my own heart towards my son. I am blown away at the thought of him loving me even half that much.

And the truth is, when my love is compared to His, it doesn't look like love at all. And it is with this so-much-greater-than-anything-like-my kind of love that He loves me.

I stand and shudder at the thought of Him loving me like that. I have nothing in my hands but gratitude.

The Lord is not slow to fulfill his promise as some count slowness, but is patient toward you, not wishing that any should perish, but that all should reach repentance. But the day of the Lord will come like a thief, and then the heavens will pass away with a roar, and the heavenly bodies will be burned up and dissolved, and the earth and the works that are done on it will be exposed. Since all these things are thus to be dissolved, what sort of people ought you to be in lives of holiness and godliness, waiting for and hastening the coming of the day of God, because of which the heavens will be set on fire and dissolved, and the heavenly bodies will melt as they burn! But according to his promise we are waiting for new heavens and a new earth in which righteousness dwells. Therefore, beloved, since you are waiting for these, be diligent to be found by him without spot or blemish, and at peace. And count the patience of our Lord as salvation, just as our beloved brother Paul also wrote to you according to the wisdom given him . . .

2 Peter 3:9-15

When are you likely to be impatient with others? How do you "tolerate" their behavior?

How is God patient with us and towards us?

List some things in this world that you wish would change?

According to 2 Peter, why doesn't God come back and start heaven today?

Who in your life do you need to approach and share the reason that you have for being patient with this world?

Additional Notes

Infection

What does it take to get your attention? I've been fighting an ear infection and struggling to hear anything clearly. It's affecting my balance, my clarity of thought, and my ability to accurately judge distance and depth.

At the end of the day, I struggle with how mentally tired I am. Primarily, because I have to pay attention to so many things that normally happen in the background.

Funnily enough, I think I am understanding things going on around me a little more clearly. I am regularly asking someone, "What did you say?" I am also evaluating whether what that person said was important enough to ask again so I can hear the exact wording used.

It is taking away so many things that are distracting for me.

How many of us are walking around needing this change in our spiritual world? How many are distracted by the many things that we hear so that we don't pay attention to the truly important things.

How has your spiritual condition impaired you? Are you off-balance, distracted, without clarity of thought, and unable to judge distance and depth?

Are you hearing sounds, but they just aren't clear? Fall into the hands of our healing Savior and watch as He removes the infection in your heart. Hopefully, you will find that the distraction helps to bring a clarity, which will remains after the healing is just a memory.

Therefore you have no excuse, O man, every one of you who judges. For in passing judgment on another you condemn yourself, because you, the judge, practice the very same things. We know that the judgment of God rightly falls on those who practice such things. Do you suppose, O man—you who judge those who practice such things and yet do them yourself—that you will escape the judgment of God? Or do you presume on the riches of his kindness and forbearance and patience, not knowing that God's kindness is meant to lead you to repentance? But because of your hard and impenitent heart you are storing up wrath for yourself on the day of wrath when God's righteous judgment will be revealed. He will render to each one according to his works: to those who by patience in well-doing seek for glory and honor and immortality, he will give eternal life; but for those who are self-seeking and do not obey the truth, but obey unrighteousness, there will be wrath and fury.

Romans 2:1-16 (cont.)

There will be tribulation and distress for every human being who does evil, the Jew first and also the Greek, but glory and honor and peace for everyone who does good, the Jew first and also the Greek. For God shows no partiality. For all who have sinned without the law will also perish without the law, and all who have sinned under the law will be judged by the law. For it is not the hearers of the law who are righteous before God, but the doers of the law who will be justified. For when Gentiles, who do not have the law, by nature do what the law requires, they are a law to themselves, even though they do not have the law. They show that the work of the law is written on their hearts, while their conscience also bears witness, and their conflicting thoughts accuse or even excuse them on that day when, according to my gospel, God judges the secrets of men by Christ Jesus.

Romans 2:1–16

What are some of the things that distract you spiritually?

What could help bring clarity for you in these areas?

List one area that you feel like you need spiritual healing in.

Will you commit to not just praying for healing in your life, but also for opportunities to sharing the story of that healing with others?

Paid in Full

We sing somewhat joyfully of the suffering Savior. We rejoice mournfully over His pain and what that means to us.

Our debt is paid in full, and the price has been paid. But we fail to grasp the enormity of this reality. We are covered not just individually, but mankind corporately has been covered.

I tend to think of how big a task it would be for one to die for my sins and what that means to me. I almost never think of the sin-debt of billions.

I seldom think of what the wrath of God towards a sinner such as myself would look like. It is too uncomfortable. I can't imagine to think for even a moment of what the wrath of God poured out for ALL the sins of ALL humanity would look like.

Jesus bore all this burden and satiated for all time the massive and completely just wrath of God.

How do we begin to adequately describe this? How do we react to one who denied Himself so much for the betterment of so many?

Do we really diminish this deed and relegate Him to the role of good man, wise teacher or even prophet? The only question worth asking, and indeed worth answering, is what have you done in response to this Man? If you are trusting in anyone or anything else but Christ, you are missing the mark by an infinite amount.

For we ourselves were once foolish, disobedient, led astray, slaves to various passions and pleasures, passing our days in malice and envy, hated by others and hating one another. But when the goodness and loving kindness of God our Savior appeared, he saved us, not because of works done by us in righteousness, but according to his own mercy, by the washing of regeneration and renewal of the Holy Spirit, whom he poured out on us richly through Jesus Christ our Savior, so that being justified by his grace we might become heirs according to the hope of eternal life.

Titus 3:3-7

What is a time or situation that made you completely aware of the massive depravity of your own soul?

How does it make you feel, knowing that Christ's righteousness is a greater good than the whole combined sin-debt of every person who has or will ever exist?

Who is the greatest sinner that you have ever personally known? What stops you from praying for their salvation?

Who is someone in your life that you are going to commit to pray for their eyes to be opened to the gospel?

What is one thing in your life that you are specifically going to trust Christ to change?

ಎಐಎಐಎಐಎಐಎಐಎಐಎಐ
Additional Notes

Alive

I sing about Christ being alive and I believe it. Yet I daily act differently. I walk around as though everything depends on me.

If I truly believed and understood this truth – that He is alive and that indeed He lives for me and in me – then my life would reflect this truth.

And while I wish in my heart that this was the case, I recognize in my head that this is not true.

I constantly miss the balance between trusting God (this often has me doing nothing), and trying too hard (this often has me trusting myself), and having faith in the face of fear while doing my part.

It seems like it requires equal parts faith, actions and understanding.

It seems clear to me if we are to err, that we should err on the side of trusting Him.

Yet even if I win the lottery, I find I have some checks to write.

Father, Son and Spirit, help me remember the truth that is the fact that You ARE alive and You care for me. Grant me wisdom in understanding what you would have me do, at the same time help me trust completely in your grace and mercy to accomplish it.

Trust in the LORD with all your heart, and do not lean on your own understanding. In all your ways acknowledge him, and he will make straight your paths.

Proverbs 3:5-6

But someone will say, "You have faith and I have works." Show me your faith apart from your works, and I will show you my faith by my works. You believe that God is one; you do well. Even the demons believe—and shudder! Do you want to be shown, you foolish person, that faith apart from works is useless? Was not Abraham our father justified by works when he offered up his son Isaac on the altar? You see that faith was active along with his works, and faith was completed by his works; and the Scripture was fulfilled that says, "Abraham believed God, and it was counted to him as righteousness"—and he was called a friend of God. You see that a person is justified by works and not by faith alone.

James 2:18-24

What stops you from trusting God with everything?

What area of your life do you wish God would get around to changing?

Is there anything you can do to help Him start that change today?

Do you struggle more with trying too hard (and trusting yourself) or being too patient (and waiting on God), as though you have no part?

What does it look like for you to strive to trust Him while continuing in your own efforts to change?

೧೩೧೩೧೩೧೩೧೩೧೩೧೩೧೩೧೩೧೩೧೩
Additional Notes

My all

What does it mean for me to give you my all? All I have was given to me, all I have was handed to me. I don't deserve anything I have. Nothing I have is original or anything for me to be proud of.

How humbling it is to have nothing and to know it. And at the same time have so much for no great deed or deeds of me or mine.

I wonder if this is what it would be like to move from an orphanage and then be adopted by a billionaire. How can you then brag on the playground about "my dad" and pretend like there is any of you in the riches with which you have been blessed.

I cannot brag of the all which I give back to You. Yet the more I have to give back, the more Your all is apparent.

Thank you, Lord, for all I have. Help me give my all to You.

And he sat down opposite the treasury and watched the people putting money into the offering box. Many rich people put in large sums. And a poor widow came and put in two small copper coins, which make a penny. And he called his disciples to him and said to them, "Truly, I say to you, this poor widow has put in more than all those who are contributing to the offering box. For they all contributed out of their abundance, but she out of her poverty has put in everything she had, all she had to live on."

Mark 12:41-44

What is the biggest gift you have ever received from someone?

How did it make you feel about the person who gave it to you?

What is the biggest gift you have ever given to someone?

Why did you give it to them?

How did their reaction to your gift make you feel? Your own reaction to giving it to them?

ଔଔଔଔଔଔଔଔଔଔଔଔ
Additional Notes

What does it mean to pray?

The simple definition I've heard is that prayer is talking with God. What does it really mean to talk with someone? To put our heart and mind in tune with them. To ask the question, how are they feeling right now? If I am really talking with someone, am I asking, "How can I line up my attitude and demeanor with them?"

How is it different to talk to a friend versus a stranger?

How does it differ when we stand before our best friend who is also a stranger?

What IS the difference between friends and strangers? Is it familiarity? Is it our behavior and/or emotions towards them? Is it their behavior and/or emotions towards us?

Who am I really a friend to? And who do I know well enough that we would equally say we are friends?

And who is a greater friend to me than Christ?

Teach us to pray. Teach us, Father.

For what great nation is there that has a god so near to it as the LORD our God is to us, whenever we call upon him? And what great nation is there, that has statutes and rules so righteous as all this law that I set before you today?

Deuteronomy 4:7-8

Truly, truly, I say to you, whoever believes in me will also do the works that I do; and greater works than these will he do, because I am going to the Father. Whatever you ask in my name, this I will do, that the Father may be glorified in the Son. If you ask me anything in my name, I will do it. If you love me, you will keep my commandments. And I will ask the Father, and he will give you another Helper, to be with you forever, even the Spirit of truth, whom the world cannot receive, because it neither sees him nor knows him. You know him, for he dwells with you and will be in you. I will not leave you as orphans; I will come to you.

John 14:12-18

What stops you from praying?

What scares you about prayer?

If you could ask God, who is able to do anything, for one thing, what would it be?

How do you think Him granting you your request would bring God glory?

If God could ask you for anything, and He was sure you would do it, what do you think He would ask?

ଔଔଔଔଔଔଔଔଔଔଔଔ
Additional Notes

End To These Troubles

There will be an end to whatever trouble is on your plate today. There is a provision that covers it completely.

My focus is so narrow and so short-sighted that when those words are spoken to me, I immediately think of today's problem. How insurmountable it seems, no matter what it is. Whether a financial burden or my hearts concern for a relational conflict in my life, or some other situation that seems equally overwhelming.

These problems are so real and need provision larger than life. Yet the Provider has given so much more than what is needed to solve this particular problem. This problem is just one of many present and one of many coming in this fallen world.

His provision covers not only temporary, earthly struggles, but also eternal spiritual ones. Sometimes He provides for the later by the former. From a temporal perspective this may seem not fair, but His foresight is limitless and His provision complete.

Praise be to the One God of the Universe, entirely worthy of Praise. Thank You for your promise that someday all problems will fade away and only Christ's glory will remain.

But I am a worm and not a man, scorned by mankind and despised by the people. All who see me mock me; they make mouths at me; they wag their heads; "He trusts in the LORD; let him deliver him; let him rescue him, for he delights in him!" Yet you are he who took me from the womb; you made me trust you at my mother's breasts. On you was I cast from my birth, and from my mother's womb you have been my God. Be not far from me, for trouble is near, and there is none to help.

Psalms 22:6-11

What is about your current problems that is so troubling for you? Do you recognize your part in them?

How do you feel toward others responsible for creating, adding to, not responding to or ignoring your current pain? Why do you think they respond that way?

Have you ever fell on your face and cried out to God over these issues? Do you think He heard you? Why do you think He hasn't done anything yet?

Can you put your faith in Him to provide? Will you commit to reaching out to someone else to share how God provides for you in this time of need?

ଔଔଔଔଔଔଔଔଔଔଔଔ
Additional Notes

I Know . . .

You are everything. Are in everything. Control everything. And are bigger than every thing.

I know . . .

I am nothing. Am not worthy. Know nothing

And cannot understand anything.

And yet You call me Yours.

You call me special and call my cries for help incense.

You chose me for things and reasons

I don't yet know and can't understand.

Your choice to make nothing become something shows the greatness of your Glory.

Whether the nothing is the darkness of space or the darkness of the life of a simple man.

When you lift me up your strength is shown.

What can stand against me when you are with me?

The depths of my doubts show the greatness of your glory.

Somehow I stand when I feel like can't even remember how to breath.

Your love clearly shines through, and it is bigger than anything I know.

But he said to me, "My grace is sufficient for you, for my power is made perfect in weakness." Therefore I will boast all the more gladly of my weaknesses, so that the power of Christ may rest upon me. For the sake of Christ, then, I am content with weaknesses, insults, hardships, persecutions, and calamities. For when I am weak, then I am strong. I have been a fool! You forced me to it, for I ought to have been commended by you. For I was not at all inferior to these super-apostles, even though I am nothing.

2 Corinthians 12:9-11

Does it feel like a cliché to say that God's grace is sufficient? How is His power made known through our weakness?

How often have you had to endure weaknesses, hardships, insults, persecutions and calamities? Were they because of something you had done? Or because of your faith in Christ?

Why does Paul say he will boast of his weaknesses?

Think of a time in your past where it seemed like you or someone close to you seemed to have no hope. How did God bring you or them through that?

ଔଔଔଔଔଔଔଔଔଔଔଔଔ

Additional Notes

Awakened

What does it mean to be awakened?

I was asleep and am now awakened.

Blind....I see.

Alone... A part of a family.

Confused...clear.

There are a million metaphors that work.

I was as asleep as any man, and now I am aware of things that in the past went without notice, barely able to even rouse a snore.

I am now aware of my snoring and my breath.

For how long did I sit in the half-dreaming/half-waking state, barely aware of what was going on around me and completely lacking any proper response?

Father keep my eyes open. Make me aware of not just my sin and my selfishness, but also my attempts at righteousness.

I cannot rouse myself. On my own, slumber is even present in my wakened state. Only through your eyes can I be aware of the "real" reality.

You are great and might and worthy of praise. Praise God from who all blessings flow.

While he was still speaking, someone from the ruler's house came and said, "Your daughter is dead; do not trouble the Teacher any more." But Jesus on hearing this answered him, "Do not fear; only believe, and she will be well." And when he came to the house, he allowed no one to enter with him, except Peter and John and James, and the father and mother of the child. And all were weeping and mourning for her, but he said, "Do not weep, for she is not dead but sleeping." And they laughed at him, knowing that she was dead. But taking her by the hand he called, saying, "Child, arise." And her spirit returned, and she got up at once. And he directed that something should be given her to eat.

Luke 8:49-55

What metaphor do you think best describes your state without Christ?

What are the first things you do when you wake up in the morning? How are they similar to things you should do as Christ awakens you?

In Luke, what is the reaction to Christ telling the family that the girl was merely sleeping? Why do you think that is?

What is the first thing that Christ tells the family to do with the girl? What do you think the significance is to that?

Christ always awakens someone for a purpose. What are you going to do today with your newfound sight?

ଔଔଔଔଔଔଔଔଔଔଔଔ
Additional Notes

All in All

We sing that Jesus paid it all. I think deeply about the words. What does it mean that He paid it all? He didn't pay most of my debt. He didn't pay part. He didn't pay for the principal, and we owe the interest.

There is nothing we can do to be more righteous. Nothing to pay Him slightly back – or to change the need we have for the massive payment required.

When He says that he paid it all we can be sure. Because He is both the Payer of the debt and the One to whom the debt is owed.

Interestingly enough, He is not saying that He will just forgive our debts without payment – which would be well within his rights.

What He says is that the debt is fully and completely paid, even if it is not paid by us.

His righteousness and justice demand payment. His love and mercy provides that required payment.

How then would we/should we respond to the One who paid our debts? How then should we live? How conscious should we be of the fact that we are loved by that payer of our debts? How aware should we be of our inadequacy and inability to pay Him back?

Our efforts should be filled with the respect due to great price paid and also filled with the knowledge that while we can't repay the debt that does not even for an instant reduce our desire to show our love and appreciation to the One who paid our debt.

Do not lie to one another, seeing that you have put off the old self with its practices and have put on the new self, which is being renewed in knowledge after the image of its creator. Here there is not Greek and Jew, circumcised and uncircumcised, barbarian, Scythian, slave, free; but Christ is all, and in all. Put on then, as God's chosen ones, holy and beloved, compassionate hearts, kindness, humility, meekness, and patience, bearing with one another and, if one has a complaint against another, forgiving each other; as the Lord has forgiven you, so you also must forgive. And above all these put on love, which binds everything together in perfect harmony.

Colossians 3:9-14

What is the largest debt you have ever owed? How would it have felt to receive a letter from the person you owed it to saying they had paid it in full?

What would it look like if all the Christians in the world forgave each other as the Lord had forgiven them?

How does displaying the positive traits described by Paul in Colossians show "putting on" our new life in Christ?

What does putting off your old self look like to you?

What is one loving thing you can do for another believer today?

൞൞൞൞൞൞൞൞൞൞൞

Additional Notes

Christ Is Risen

I struggle with lyrics. I have found myself in the past so willing to proclaim what I will do for God, how I will praise Him and I will sing to Him, or how I will proclaim Him.

After examining both my actions and my heart, I have found myself failing. This has caused me to hesitate to proclaim these things.

Today, I have found my sin is an unwillingness to proclaim anything that I would do. I am fearful of failing again to live up to my "proclamations" again. I always want to make sure the focus of any action is to recognize that Christ is the one doing it.

While singing lyrics I'm constantly asking, "What is this saying? Who is doing what in this song?" Regularly I find that the song is saying what "I" or "we" will do. And this is a part of my struggle. I've discovered my own inability to do anything I desire reliably.

In a song recently, I discovered a line about Christ. It says "Christ has risen, Christ is living and He will come again." As I meditated on this, I realized that this not merely a statement of what has happened, is happening or will happen, but it is also a statement of who it is that accomplished these things.

Christ didn't just rise. He himself caused His resurrection. It didn't happen to Him. He did it. He isn't on loan from death or Hell. Hell itself couldn't contain Him. He was in His very nature MORE than the grave. It wasn't large enough to contain Him. He was WAY too big for it.

He is coming again. Let me repeat that. The Divine Representation of God in human form will return to this planet once again. Yet this time in a way revealing the same glory and power that He has always had and will always have.

Christ has risen. Christ is still risen. And Christ will return, as alive as He has ever been.

Think over what I say, for the Lord will give you understanding in everything. Remember Jesus Christ, risen from the dead, the offspring of David, as preached in my gospel, for which I am suffering, bound with chains as a criminal. But the word of God is not bound!

2 Timothy 2:7-9

But the angel said to the women, "Do not be afraid, for I know that you seek Jesus who was crucified. He is not here, for he has risen, as he said. Come, see the place where he lay."

Matthew 28:5-6

What does it mean to you that God is the one with the power to cause His own resurrection?

What should our response be to a God who loves us enough to suffer for us?

What would you say to that God if you were face-to-face with Him?

What would it mean to you for Him to tell you that you were specially made to serve a special purpose and that He was proud of your role that you have played for Him?

☙☙☙☙☙☙☙☙☙☙☙☙

Additional Notes

Declared the King

When I declare You king, what do I mean?

Do I declare, or proclaim You some son of some son who once had power?

Do I declare You someone that we can hold up as a celebrity and someone to admire? Are You the shadow of power that once existed in some former world that has long since faded away?

Or do I declare Your right to both reign and rule in my world and also in my own personal life? Do I declare Your right to command me and order me to do battle for You or send me to the gallows for my offenses against You?

Do I proclaim my undying devotion due to One of supreme magnificence and glory, or do I merely mean that I will look in Your general direction once a week for as much as an hour at a time?

Father, forgive my declarations of Your divinity and authority. You do not need me to be King. You do not need my praise in order for You to be God.

Help my heart, mind and soul declare what IS true of You with no pretending that it is somehow truer because I believe it.

Help me to see and be more aware of the reality that is and to point others to it, no matter what that means for me and my earthly or eternal position.

Thank you for being authoritative.

Who is this King of glory? The LORD, strong and mighty, the LORD, mighty in battle! Lift up your heads, O gates! And lift them up, O ancient doors, that the King of glory may come in. Who is this King of glory? The LORD of hosts, he is the King of glory! Selah.

Psalms 24:8-10

Is there anyone that you have admired or appreciated that would be considered famous or important?

How do you feel when you are around someone of great power or celebrity?

How would it make you feel if that important person decided to ask you if they could spend an afternoon with you?

What would you request from or want to communicate with someone of such great power and insight?

What stops you from doing so with God?

ଔଔଔଔଔଔଔଔଔଔଔଔ

Additional Notes

Sin Forgiven

It is easy to minimize sin.

Easy to compare my sins to others.

Easy to win the war of someone else is worse than me.

But it is impossible to measure up to perfection.

We find it easy to accept the saying that says, "No one is perfect."

We mistakenly accept that saying as if it is describing what ought to be and don't recognize it as merely a statement of fact.

As we discover the depths of our depravity, we should be overwhelmed by the immenseness of God's provision.

It should bother us on a cosmic level that our need is not just large but it is infinite.

It should also comfort us on a cosmic level that our provision is infinitely larger. We can rest in the words that tell us our sin is forgiven.

And every priest stands daily at his service, offering repeatedly the same sacrifices, which can never take away sins. But when Christ had offered for all time a single sacrifice for sins, he sat down at the right hand of God, waiting from that time until his enemies should be made a footstool for his feet. For by a single offering he has perfected for all time those who are being sanctified. And the Holy Spirit also bears witness to us; for after saying, "This is the covenant that I will make with them after those days, declares the Lord: I will put my laws on their hearts, and write them on their minds," then he adds, "I will remember their sins and their lawless deeds no more." Where there is forgiveness of these, there is no longer any offering for sin.

Hebrews 10:11-18

O foolish Galatians! Who has bewitched you? It was before your eyes that Jesus Christ was publicly portrayed as crucified. Let me ask you only this: Did you receive the Spirit by works of the law or by hearing with faith? Are you so foolish? Having begun by the Spirit, are you now being perfected by the flesh? Did you suffer so many things in vain—if indeed it was in vain? Does he who supplies the Spirit to you and works miracles among you do so by works of the law, or by hearing with faith—just as Abraham "believed God, and it was counted to him as righteousness"? Know then that it is those of faith who are the sons of Abraham. And the Scripture, foreseeing that God would justify the Gentiles by faith, preached the gospel beforehand to Abraham, saying, "In you shall all the nations be blessed."

Galatians 3:1-8

How often do you find yourself comparing your deeds with others? Find yourself thinking about how "bad" someone else's deeds are, particularly when listening to the evening news?

Do you ever live with regret from past sins? How does the thought that God will, "remember their deeds no more" make you feel?

How does it feel when you think about the fact that both your sins and God's provision for them are infinite?

What is something you can do to show the same forgiveness that you've received with someone that you know that has wronged you?

Additional Notes

Conclusions

His plan for us involves stress, and other-worldly provision.

Final Thoughts

I hope that you have found these passages both helpful and challenging. I hope that they relieved stress when you were overly stressful and that they have also caused stress when you were too comfortable.

You may have noticed the similarity to these verses and many of David's laments in Psalms. I think this is true, because it is the nature of life and sinfulness for us to doubt and wonder. And at the end of the day, we should always find ourselves back firmly in the hands of a loving God. We should not be bothered when it takes more than a day or a week or a month to get to "the end of the day."

He is no less present during our doubts. He is no less aware when I hide in the darkness. He is no less loving when I feel utterly alone. He is no less powerful when it appears like He is not changing anything.

Cast your cares on a God who is more than large enough to handle them. You may have to start the conversation with tough questions. You may need to share with Him the anger, frustration or pain that you feel today. Maybe you start by sharing about all the pain you felt yesterday and still haven't gotten over.

Be assured, He can handle your tough questions. He is not worried that you will stump Him. He is not worried that your sin will be too deep for His provision to cover.

He is not trying to figure out where to get enough money to pay for your current debts. He is not wishing that he understood a little bit more about cancer or whatever other physical ailments you may have so He can heal. He is not confused or perplexed at all by your situation. He isn't trying to figure out how this is all going to work out. He is not puzzled by why this is happening now.

Turn and face the God who is chasing after you, and you will find an embrace that comforts like no other. His plan for us involves stress, as well as other-worldly provision.

If you need anything you may reach out to me, but more importantly please reach out to Him.

Mitch

And let us not grow weary of doing good, for in due season we will reap, if we do not give up. So then, as we have opportunity, let us do good to everyone, and especially to those who are of the household of faith.

Gal 6:9-10

Afterword

This book came to be because for the longest time I have responded to worship and music with verse. These passages used to get scribbled on bulletins, but in recent years have been typed into my cellphone.

The big advantage is that I can call them back up much more conveniently, and it makes it much easier to share with others when the conversation seems appropriate.

The big disadvantage is that it often looks like I am texting instead of worshipping.

So the bulk of this writing is a compilation of things that I've composed in response to worship at my church.

I will occasionally pull out my phone while having a conversation with someone about God and share one of these verses. Their response is usually, "Who wrote that?" as though they are expecting the answer to be Spurgeon or some great thinker. I struggle to reply, "It was me," and try to skip past their comments; however after receiving this response over and over again, I began to think that I should put them down in some format.

As I did so and started reviewing these writings, I received so much benefit from re-reading these and I thought it was time to share them with the world.

I'd been trying to come up with a good description for this writing and found it was a great struggle for me. But as I did this I started to discover something about both these writings in addition to something about me.

I was looking for a way to describe something both poetic and deep, but also something both bare, and yet layered while remaining strong and still vulnerable. I struggled to come up with some way to describe the variety of things to expect from my writing.

While thinking of a way to describe something poetic the word "iambic" crossed my mind and it stuck. For those of you who aren't familiar with the word iambic, (and didn't read about it in the beginning of the book), it is a literary word used to describe the rhythm of unstressed and stressed syllables in poetry. It is most famous in the poetic writing of Shakespeare, who wrote in iambic pentameter.

As I looked at the metaphor deeper, I find my life seems like this series of unstressed and then stressed moments. My soul responds to both emotions accordingly. In truth, I typically rebel against the stress and deny that it "should" be present in my life.

I believe the lie that says that stress is bad and that the unstressed times are what life here on Earth should be like. Much of what I write reflects the balance of stressed and unstressed thoughts and emotions I frequently have.

In these pages you should have found words from my heart and beyond. These thoughts often reflect a more complete thought and more raw emotion than I am usually prone to share.

They are not intended to be poems, yet many are poetic.

Some express theological thoughts. Some are pure praise. Many are in response to a single line in a worship song. Many in response to the many stresses of life.

These were written during a time of great stress for my family, as we struggled, financially, relationally, spiritually and directionally for a long period of time. At the same time my life during this writing was also filled with so many great joys.

The intended audience was me and my Savior. I think I got more out of it than He did, but His response to the praise of His children is probably more relevant than any of my own thoughts or responses.

I have found the words encouraging, convicting, challenging and thought-provoking. Hopefully they have encouraged you as much as they have me.

Thank you again for reading.

I can do all things through him who strengthens me.

Philippians 4:13

About the Author

Mitch Comstock has written many blogs and articles for several websites and magazines and is a regular contributor to the Nashville Christian Family magazine.

He attends the Bridge Church in Spring Hill, Tennessee.

Mitch is a board member and regular attendee at the Tennessee Christian Chamber of Commerce events.

He owns Legendary Computers, a computer repair and service company in Franklin, Tennessee, and is a regular speaker and trainer on a variety of subjects.

He has a bachelor's degree in Mass Communication from Wright State University in Dayton, Ohio.

He lives in Spring Hill with his wife Misti and is the father to 4 very energetic sons.

To read more about his spiritual thoughts and journey visit iambicsoul.com

To schedule speaking engagements for Mitch either as a LinkedIn/Social Media/Technology Speaker/Trainer or to schedule him to speak about life/love/liberty and the awe-inspiring grace of God contact:

Lee Porter at Aspiring Mark Agency.

615-656-5987 or lporter@aspiringmark.com

Made in the USA
Monee, IL
07 April 2022

94308996R00111